CONTENTS

Should Dogs Be Banned from the Beach?

Dogs on Beaches Cause Outrage

Tuesday, 2 October

Local residents are outraged by the number of dogs allowed to roam on beaches.

They feel that owners need to take greater responsibility for their animals. A local action group has approached the council with a petition to have dogs banned from the beach.

Predict:

What do you think the arguments for and against dogs being banned from the beach might be?

Clarify:

petition

A a small pet

B a written request
   by lots of people

C something that is repeated

A, B or C?

BAN DOGS FROM THE BEACH

BAN DOGS FROM THE BEACH

Letters to the Editor

Wednesday, 3 October

Dogs have feelings, too!

Yesterday I read with interest your report about banning dogs from beaches. I strongly believe dogs should be allowed on the beach. Healthy dogs need exercise. Long walks along the beach give them the opportunity to stretch their legs. However, their owners should keep them on a leash. The petition by the local community seems an overreaction to the problem. It's the owners of the dogs who need to take more responsibility for their pets. Don't blame the dog!

Amy Bembok, Sunnysands

From the kennel …

Dogs need freedom just as much as people do. Dogs running along the beach and swimming in the surf are lovely to watch. I have bred dogs for more than 20 years, and exercise is the best way of keeping a dog fit and healthy. Well-trained dogs cause no problems on the beach at all.

David Cheong, Sunnysands

Abide by beach rules with your dog

Keep dogs away from our beaches. Hundreds of people use the beach for recreation each day. They need to be able to walk and play freely without being annoyed by roaming dogs. Dogs also frighten the local wildlife. They chase seagulls as they are feeding, causing the birds a great deal of stress. People should keep their dogs at home where they can be easily supervised.

Frederick Peters, Stockton

Clarify:

what does the term

ABIDE BY BEACH RULES...

mean?

FACT OR OPINION?

FACT =

A statement that can be proved to be true

OPINION =

A view or belief that is not based on fact or knowledge

- Dogs running along the beach and swimming in the surf are lovely to watch.

- Exercise is the best way of keeping a dog fit and healthy.

- It's the owners of the dogs who need to take more responsibility for their pets.

- Dogs need freedom just as much as people do.

Don't let your dog be a danger!

Keep dogs off the beach, I say! I can't believe how inconsiderate pet owners can be about the rights of other people! We all know dogs ruin the beach for others. Only last week my son stuck his hand into dog droppings while he was building a sand castle. Surely this shouldn't happen in this day and age. Dogs also dig holes that can be dangerous to people walking on the beach. We don't want an elderly person being injured by accidentally tripping in a hole. If people want pets, they should keep them at home.

Maria Spinoli, Belmont

Taking the lead on dog behaviour

Many people are concerned about dogs running loose on the beach, but banning them is not the answer. Dogs and humans both need exercise. Locking dogs up is not a solution.

Most problems can be overcome by common sense. Plastic bags and special bins should be provided so owners can clean up any dog droppings. People should fill in holes dug by their pets. Owners could also take their dogs to obedience classes. If people followed these simple solutions, the beach would be safe for everyone and dogs could be happy, too.

Carlos Cornelius, Black Stump

Clarify: inconsiderate

A informal

B careful

C thoughtless

A, B or C?

Question:

Now that you have read both sides of the argument, what do you think? Which side do you agree with?

SUMMARY

Opinion 1.

Dogs **should** be banned from the beach.

What are the main arguments to support this opinion?

Opinion 2.

Dogs **should not** be banned from the beach.

What are the main arguments to support this opinion?

Should the Toy Factory Be Built Near Marshland?

Toy factory for Sunside creates community debate

Thursday, 4 October

Bigtime Developments plan to construct a new toy factory on the land between Tarro Road and Duff Creek. If the project goes ahead, it will be the biggest development in Sunside for the past 50 years.

The majority of councillors welcomed the toy factory as a positive for unemployed people. Building the factory will take about ten months, and will employ many workers. Once the factory is built, it will create 100 permanent jobs as well as supporting many small businesses in the area.

However, several people have expressed concern about the factory's environmental impact on the marshland habitat around the area.

A model of the planned development can be viewed in the foyer of council chambers. Objections to the proposal must be made in writing within 30 days.

Predict:

What do you think the arguments for and against the toy factory being built might be?

Letters to the Editor

Friday, 5 October

Save the water hen

I was shocked to read that the new toy factory might be built near the creek. Not only is this area a feeding ground for many birds and small animals, it is the breeding ground for the water hen. The swampland simply must not be filled in. Besides deliberately destroying habitat, the factory may cause toxic chemicals to be released accidentally into the creek. This would cause much damage to the environment.

Any councillors who vote for this factory will answer for their actions at the next elections.

Belle Blinman, Greenwoods

Inference:

Any councillors that vote for this factory will answer for their actions at the next elections.

What inferences can be made from this comment?

Don't pollute the patients!

Council should not be rushing the toy factory project through in such a hurry. We live along Tarro Road and oppose the building of a factory so close to our homes. Some of us sleep during the day because we are shift-workers at the hospital. Not only will noise from the factory keep us awake, but the extra traffic of heavy trucks past our front doors will be unbearable. We are not the only ones who will be affected. Patients at the hospital will also suffer from the factory's noise and pollution. Build it on a more suitable site!

The Redman, Chang and King families, Sunside

Support the toys!

Everyone should support the proposal for the new toy factory. It's about time something was done to help the unemployed. The high cost of benefits means that we are paying more and more taxes. It's difficult for the unemployed to survive under the present conditions. The sooner the factory is built, the better.

Theo Valla, Stockton

Give the factory the go-ahead!

At last the council is doing something to help the unemployed! They've done the right thing in encouraging Bigtime Developments to come to our town. I've been unemployed for one year and can't wait for the factory to be built, as it will hopefully mean a job for me. I'm a single father, and bringing up two children on unemployment benefits is extremely difficult. The council deserves a pat on the back.

Lars Milan, Sunside

Town needs a new industry

Our town desperately needs a new industry. As well as easing our unemployment problem, the toy factory proposed by Bigtime Developments would bring workers willing to spend money to our town. Disadvantages such as noise, loss of the marshland habitat, and the risk of pollution are minimal compared to the benefits the factory will bring to our community. The dispute will have to be settled quickly or Bigtime may go to another town.

Leilani Matai, Sunnybrook

Question:

Now that you have read both sides of the argument, what do you think? Which side do you agree with?

SUMMARY

Opinion 1.

The toy factory
should not be built.

What are the main arguments to
support this opinion?

Opinion 2.

The toy factory **should** be built.

What are the main arguments to
support this opinion?

WHAT DO YOU THINK?

Should Cats Be Locked Up at Night?

Curfew for Killer Cats

Monday, 8 October

Members of the local cat club were distressed to hear that the council is considering introducing a night-time curfew for cats.

Conservation groups interested in preserving the local environment and wildlife have been fighting for such a move for some time. Now a new study supports their statement that cats kill more birds and small animals than most people believe.

For the past year, Professor Lani Lawson from the National University has been researching the effect cats have on wildlife. At a public meeting yesterday, she said that most cats kill even when they are not hungry. When a small animal moves, a cat will pounce on it instinctively.

Several cat owners are cooperating in the research by keeping details of their own cats' activities. Most owners thought their pets stayed close to home. They were amazed when small transmitters attached to their cats' collars showed how far they roamed.

Clarify: curfew

A an order stopping people or animals going out after a set time

B a bird that lives on the seashore

C the ringing of a bell at a set time

A, B or C?

Predict:

What do you think the arguments for and against cats being locked up at night might be?

Letters to the Editor

Tuesday, 9 October

Cruelty to cats is not on!

Being a cat owner, I read Professor Lawson's report with interest. I feel it's extremely cruel to lock cats up at night. They are night-time animals, and it is natural for them to roam after dark. My cat has a bell on her collar, and this warns any bird or small animal that she is near. It's unfair to punish responsible pet owners just because others let their cats run wild.

Katarina Karonie, Greenwoods

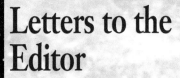

Antonym

cruel

Think of an antonym.

Antonym = A word opposite in meaning to another word

Set cats free!

Professor Lawson seems to think the simple answer to protecting the wildlife is to lock cats up at night. While some cats may kill a few birds, it is not practical to lock all cats up at night. Cats need to run about to stay fit and healthy, just as other animals do. My cat stays in the house while I am at work, and I let her out when I come home. As it is almost dark by this time, she is often free for a little while after sunset. Is she going to be picked up by the council? What am I supposed to do – lock her up 24 hours a day?

Glendon Flaxley, Sunnysands

Synonym

protecting

Think of a synonym.

Synonym = A word or a phrase with a meaning similar to another word or phrase

Love your pets – lock them up!

Cats in my neighbourhood drive me mad. Professor Lawson has made a good case for keeping cats in at night, but protecting the wildlife is not the only reason. Cat fights and loud miaowing often keep me awake. Last week there was an accident outside my house when a motorist swerved to avoid a cat. It's about time someone made irresponsible cat owners realise what trouble their pets cause to others. If people value their pets, they should close them in at night.

Buck Hedley, Sunnysands

Take responsibility!

Scientific evidence shows that cats kill birds and small animals, so it's obvious that cats and wildlife must be kept apart. Responsible people already make sure their pets are inside after dark, but there are some who, for whatever reason, don't do this. When the actions of a few people have such an effect on our environment and cause unnecessary problems for other people, it is time the council took a firm stand and enforced a curfew on cats.

Sylvia Englebert, Jacksonville

Question:

Now that you have read both sides of the argument, what do you think? Which side do you agree with?

SUMMARY

Opinion 1.

Cats <u>should not</u>
be locked up at night.

What are the main arguments to
support this opinion?

Opinion 2.

Cats <u>should</u> be locked up at night.

What are the main arguments to
support this opinion?

THINK ABOUT THE TEXT

Making connections – What connections can you make to the events explored in *What Do You Think?*

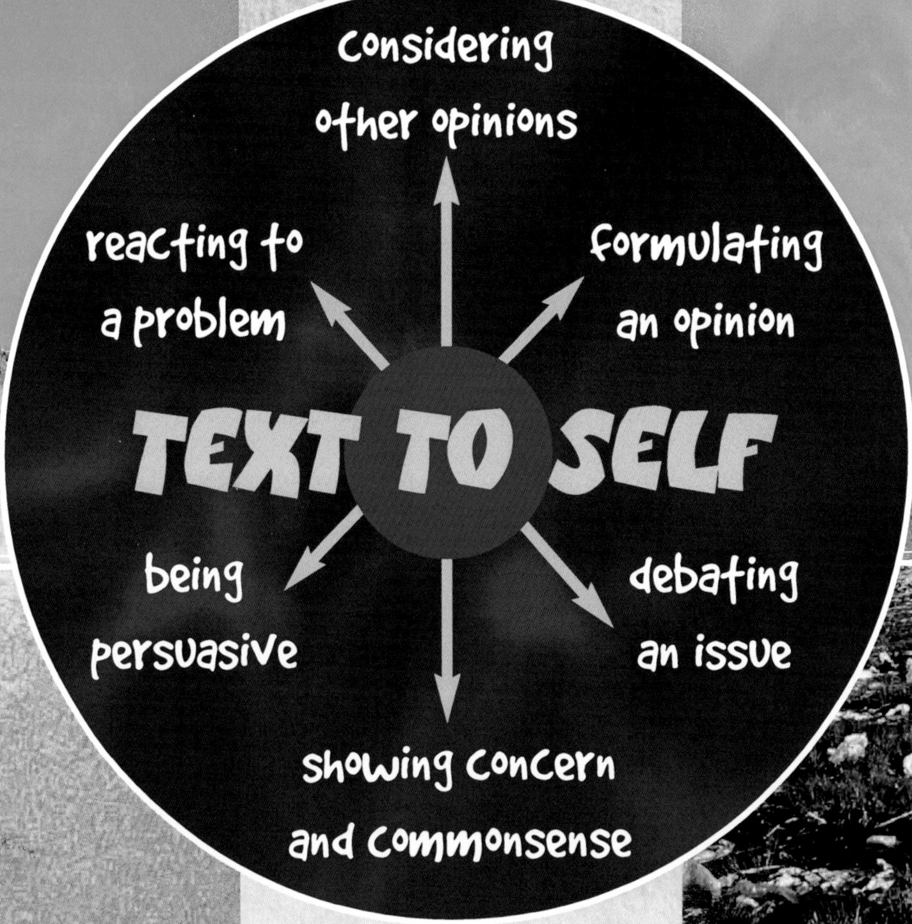

Considering other opinions

reacting to a problem

formulating an opinion

TEXT TO SELF

being persuasive

debating an issue

showing concern and commonsense

TEXT TO TEXT

Talk about other letters to the editor you have read that have similar features to those in *What Do You Think?* Compare the texts.

TEXT TO WORLD

Talk about situations in the world that might connect to elements in the text.

PLANNING A LETTER TO THE EDITOR

1

Select an issue you have read about in a magazine or newspaper that is causing you concern

2

Decide which viewpoints of the issue you agree or disagree with

3

Make an opening statement in which you identify the issue and state your own viewpoint strongly

Taking the lead on dog behaviour

Many people are concerned about dogs running loose on the beach, but banning them is not the answer. Dogs and humans both need exercise. Locking dogs up is not a solution.

4

Give some reasons or examples that support your point of view

Most problems can be overcome by common sense. Plastic bags and special bins should be provided so owners can clean up any dog droppings. People should fill in holes dug by their pets. Owners could also take their dogs to obedience classes.

A LETTER TO THE EDITOR

A Is written in the first person.

B Uses short paragraphs and sentences.

C States the writer's opinion strongly.

D Uses quotes, examples and facts to support the viewpoint.

E Uses emotive words to convey the writer's feelings.

F May be serious or humorous or convey sarcasm or anger.

G Can conclude with the writer's real or made-up name and location.